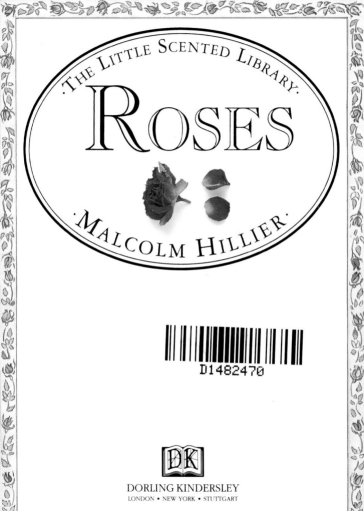

·THE LITTLE SCENTED LIBRARY·

# ROSES

·MALCOLM HILLIER·

D1482470

**DORLING KINDERSLEY**
LONDON • NEW YORK • STUTTGART

A DORLING KINDERSLEY BOOK

•

SERIES EDITORS  HEATHER DEWHURST, MARY LAMBERT
PROJECT EDITOR  SUSAN THOMPSON
ART EDITOR  CAROL McCLEEVE
MANAGING EDITOR  JANE LAING
SENIOR ART EDITOR  DAVID ROBINSON
PRODUCTION  MERYL SILBERT
PHOTOGRAPHY  MATTHEW WARD

•

FIRST PUBLISHED IN GREAT BRITAIN IN 1991
BY DORLING KINDERSLEY LIMITED,
9 HENRIETTA STREET, LONDON WC2E 8PS

•

COPYRIGHT © 1991 DORLING KINDERSLEY LIMITED, LONDON
TEXT COPYRIGHT © 1991 MALCOLM HILLIER

**2**

•

A CIP CATALOGUE RECORD FOR THIS BOOK IS AVAILABLE FROM THE BRITISH LIBRARY

•

ISBN 0-86318-561-4

•

COMPUTER PAGE MAKE-UP BY THE COOLING BROWN PARTNERSHIP
REPRODUCED BY COLOURSCAN, SINGAPORE
PRINTED IN HONG KONG

# CONTENTS

# INTRODUCTION

THE ROSE IS THE MOST BEAUTIFUL of all flowers. For two thousand years and more, roses have been the universal symbol of beauty and love, displaying their cascades of colourful flowers and voluptuous scents in gardens and homes throughout the world. Many of the most beautifully perfumed roses, such as the damasks, gallicas, bourbons, and rugosas, which were bred over the last three hundred years, had one burst of flowers in early summer and some a less prolific autumn flowering as well. Now breeders are developing new varieties of rose with all the "old rose" qualities of shape, form, and exquisite fragrance, but which flower perpetually from summer until late in the autumn.

When roses are in full bloom, the most magical place to be is in a rose garden. There the senses are bombarded with the glorious colours, shapes and perfumes of the flowers. And we can easily enjoy all of these attributes indoors. It takes no more than a single rose in a vase, a bowl of fragrant pot pourri, a deliciously scented perfume or soap, or a delectable sweetmeat to take us back into that wonderfully perfumed garden at any time we wish.

# CHOOSING ROSES

HERE ARE THOUSANDS of different garden roses to choose from and all of them are beautiful. My favourites are the ones that look old-fashioned, whether they are genuine old roses or the new "old roses" that have a long flowering season. It is more difficult to find the florists' roses that are strongly perfumed, but some, such as Parfuma and Oceana, do possess delicious scents.

**Ferdinand Pichard** has striped crimson petals and a strong scent.

**Tiffany** is a hybrid tea rose with a very rich scent and interesting salmon-gold colouring.

**Chapeau de Napoleon** has a fruity fragrance.

**Desprez à Fleur Jaune** has deliciously scented flowers.

**Portland** rose has strongly fragrant semi-double flowers.

**Charles de Mills** is a "gallica" rose with the best rose scent of all.

**Rosa Glauca** has distinctive pinky-grey foliage.

**Fountain** is a shrub rose that produces a succession of rich crimson, perfumed flowers.

**Porcelain** is a multiflora rose with pale pink, silky-textured flowers and a honey scent.

**Amber Queen** produces amber flowers with a strong fragrance.

**Honorine de Brabant** has a raspberry scent.

# PICKING ROSES

**Picking a perfect rose**

**PREPARING A ROSE**

*W*HETHER YOU pick your roses from the garden or buy them from a florist, it is worth carrying out a few simple preparations to help make them last as long as possible. When picking from the garden, choose strong-stemmed buds that are just beginning to open. If you buy roses from a shop, make sure that they have strong stems and unblemished buds.

*1* Before arranging, remove thorns and any leaves that will be below the water, to prevent rotting.

*2* Cut the stem base at an angle and scrape away 5 cm (2 in) of the stem for fast water uptake.

### TEAPOT OF ROSES
*A simple display consisting mostly
of old-fashioned roses in a teapot.
Add bleach and sugar to the water
to prolong the life of the flowers.*

# OLD-FASHIONED POSIES

*S*WEETLY SCENTED POSIES and tussie mussies make beautiful gifts, and are all the more special for being short-lived. They can convey a hidden message too. Different coloured roses mean different things, mostly relating to love, but yellow roses stand for jealousy.

### LOVER'S POSY
*This posy contains a deliciously perfumed combination of red roses for love and phlox for unanimity.*

## HIDDEN MESSAGE

*This posy, with its mixture of pink and red roses, lavender and scented geranium leaves, tells of love after a meeting.*

## TALE OF WOE

*Yellow and peach roses nestle amongst strongly scented rue leaves in this charming tussie mussie. But its appearance is particularly deceptive as its combination of flowers spell out a bold message of jealousy, perplexity and grief to the recipient.*

# COLOURFUL MIXTURES

*T*HERE ARE ROSES IN MOST COLOURS of the rainbow, though blue is still eluding the breeders. In the rose garden there are no colours that clash and it is the same with arrangements, so don't feel timid about mixing colours. Brightly coloured flowers add an interesting vibrancy to an arrangement. Try mixing all the pinks or pink and orange, or yellow, lilac and peach. Choose either contrasting or matching containers for your roses. The best containers lead the eye up to the display.

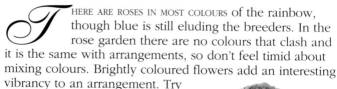

### SIMPLE ARRANGEMENT
*A blue and mauve trumpet vase takes the eye up to a simple arrangement which includes the fragrant blooms of Aloha, Roseraie de l'Hay, and Parfuma roses.*

### TREE OF ROSES
*A branch set into a
terracotta pot holds a
wet foam ball that is
first wrapped in chicken
wire and then studded
with lots of little orange
and pink roses and
alchemilla flowers.*

# LARGE DISPLAYS

**R**OSES FROM THE GARDEN tend to have short stems, whereas roses from a florist frequently have long stems. Long-stemmed roses are ideal for using in larger arrangements, such as ones that might stand on a side table, in front of a fireplace, or on a pedestal for a party. Use roses with a strong, heady fragrance, for a rose without a scent is just a pale shadow of its perfumed relations. To achieve the best effect in your display, arrange long-stemmed roses with some softer, more delicate foliage and other contrasting flowers, to break up the rather rigid look created by the straight, upright lines of the stems of the roses.

### ROSE CENTREPIECE

*A large vine basket plays host to the richly scented roses Oceana, Friendship, and Mountbatten in peach, pink, and yellow. An airy froth of mock orange, fennel, and cow parsley softens the overall effect.*

# GARLANDS

F OR A VERY SPECIAL occasion create beautiful fresh-flower garlanding to edge a buffet table, or wind around a door, window frame, or banister rail. With well-conditioned roses, the garlanding will last for about twelve hours.

**1** Prepare little bunches of flowers for the garland. Unreel mossing wire (obtainable from florists) to the length of the garland required. Make a secure loop at each end to fix the finished garland in place.

2 Lay a bunch over one end of the main wire, so it overlaps the loop, and attach it to the main wire with two twists of mossing wire. Take the wire behind the bunch. Continue binding the garland until the main wire is covered.

3 Once all the flowers are fixed firmly in position, wind strands of the decorative foliage, smilax, around the garland, working from the same direction. This will add greenery to the finished garland.

### GARLAND OF ROSES

*A decorative garland consisting of yellow and white roses, lady's mantle, and trails of smilax.*

# BOUQUETS & CIRCLETS

*A*S AN EMBLEM OF LOVE, roses have been part of the wedding ceremony for centuries. The form of the rose is perfect for bouquets; overblown flowers with petals that are nearly falling have a wonderful shape and so too have the furled buds. Especially beautiful colour combinations of roses include all white, ivory and cream, and pink and lilac.

## WEDDING ROSES

*The bride's bouquet (opposite) is made of perfumed pink, peach, and lemon yellow roses, with rose geranium and lady's mantle leaves. The bridesmaid's circlet (below) is a heart made of birch twigs and miniature amber and orange roses.*

# AIR-DRYING

MANY VARIETIES OF ROSE air-dry extremely well, the best having firm, hybrid tea-shaped flowers that are not too large. Old-fashioned and single-flowered roses should be dried using a desiccant (see pages 22-23). If you pick your own roses for drying, pick them on a dry day after any dew has evaporated. Choose roses with firm buds that are just about to open.

To air-dry roses, you will need a dark, dry, cool place where there is plenty of ventilation, as the drying process works best if it is gradual. Hang the roses either singly or in small bunches from a strand of wire, a rail, or a hook on a wall. Once they are hung, the roses will continue to open for three or four days. The drying process will then take about two weeks.

**AIR-DRYING ROSES**

*1* Use firm roses and remove all thorns and lower leaves.

*2* Tie the roses together with string, leaving a hanging loop.

### HANGING ROSES

*Hang the roses in a staggered line to allow the air to circulate.*

# PRESERVING

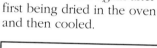

*P*RESERVING ROSES WITH A DESICCANT, such as silica gel, borax, alum, and sand, gives beautiful results and lets you dry roses that are unsuitable for air-drying. The roses must be open rather than in bud so that the crystals can surround and cover all the surfaces. The desiccant you use must be absolutely dry. Drying in silica gel takes two days, in alum and borax, ten days, and in sand, three to four weeks. Each desiccant can be used again after first being dried in the oven and then cooled.

## PRESERVING WITH DESICCANT

*1* Place silica gel in a container. Push a stub wire into the base of each rose head. Place on the gel.

*2* Carefully spoon the crystals over the roses. Seal the container and leave for 48 hours.

### DRIED ROSES

Any fully opened roses can be
dried using a desiccant.
Choose roses that are double or
single, old-fashioned with
many petals, or
the newer
multi-
floras, and
in any and
every colour.

### SWEET SCENT

Even when they are
dried, roses retain
some of their
perfume, especially
the sweeter
scented
ones.

### DECORATION

Use dried roses as
decoration for
pot pourris.

# DRIED DISPLAYS

*A* BOUQUET OF DRIED ROSES combined with other dried flowers can make a thoughtful birthday or anniversary present, or it can make an attractive decoration to hang on the wall. Dried roses retain a subtle, musky rose scent and their rich colours add depth to any arrangement of dried flowers. Make sure that any dried display is placed away from strong, bright sunlight, which will cause the colours to fade.

### GOLDEN BOUQUET
The bouquet (opposite), which glows with the mellow tones of yellow, consists of golden roses, batchelors' buttons, everlasting flowers, and eucalyptus leaves, trimmed with yellow satin ribbon. It can be given as a gift or hung on the wall.

### VIBRANT ARRANGEMENT
Dried roses displayed with cornflowers and glycerined ivy leaves can look very colourful.

# MAKING POT POURRI

*T*HE LITERAL TRANSLATION of pot pourri is "rotten pot". Originally applied to a meat stew, it became the term applied to fragrant mixtures of sweetly scented petals, herbs, and spices that were used to ward off unpleasant smells in the eighteenth century. With their warm, lingering scent, rose petals have always been a main ingredient of pot pourris.

*Rose petals*

*Coarse salt*

*Rose petals*

*Lemon verbena leaves*

*Ground cinnamon*

*Brown sugar*

*Cinnamon sticks*

*Lemon oil*

*Ground orris root*

*Rose oil*

*Cloves*

## ROSE POT POURRI

Layer 1 litre (1 qt) of fragrant
rose petals with 250 ml (8 fl oz)
each of lemon verbena leaves
and coarse salt in a crock, and
leave in a dry place for two
weeks, stirring daily. Next add
2 tablespoons each of ground
cinnamon, ground cloves,
brown sugar, and ground orris
root, and 4 drops each of rose
and lemon oil. Stir to blend the
ingredients. Seal in a crock
and store for two months.

# POT POURRIS

TRADITIONALLY, pot pourris were kept in containers with perforated lids to conserve their scent. These days we prefer pot pourri to serve a decorative role in the house. Any interesting containers with a reasonable depth can be used. Relating the colour of the pot pourri to its container strengthens the visual appeal.

### FRUITY ROSE MIX

*Mix 1 litre (1 qt) rose petals, 500 ml (1 pt) marigold petals, 250 ml (8 fl oz) blackcurrant leaves, grated rind of 4 limes, 125 ml (4 fl oz) vetiver root, 250 ml (8 fl oz) salt, and 3 drops each of rose and rose geranium oil.*

### SPICY ROSE MIXES

*For a pungent pot pourri (top left), combine 750 ml (28 fl oz) rose petals, 250 ml (8 fl oz) chamomile, 125 ml (4 fl oz) each of coltsfoot and oakmoss, and 2 drops each of bergamot and rose oil. To make a spicier pot pourri (bottom left), mix 1.5 litres (2¹/2 pt) rose petals, 250 ml (8 fl oz) ground bay, 1 tablespoon each of allspice and ground orris root, and 3 drops of rose oil.*

# SCENTED SACHETS

*R*OSE-SCENTED SACHETS AND BAGS are deliciously fragrant and can fill your bedroom and bathroom with their gentle perfume. Place a sachet between your clothes in a chest, or in a dressing-table drawer. Hang one or two from a rail, or hook one over a coat hanger in your wardrobe. Another ideal place to hang a sachet is from a bathroom cabinet. Most lightweight fabrics, such as cotton, voile, net or linen, are suitable for making into sachets, though open-weave materials, such as muslin and lace, will lose their scent faster than a close-weave silk or cotton.

## MAKING A SCENTED SACHET

*1* Cut out 2 fabric rectangles 20 x 10 cm (9 x 5 in) and stitch them together along 3 sides. Edge the open top with lace.

*2* Fill the sachet two-thirds full with a perfumed mix of rose petals, cinnamon, and rose oil. Close the sachet with a ribbon.

31

## ROSY SACHET

*This sachet has been made in a complementary glazed cotton and tied with a pretty matching ribbon. Use your sachets to decorate a dressing table or bathroom shelf, where their rosy perfume will scent the air with a lasting fragrance.*

# PERFUMED SOAPS

*R*OSES MAKE A DELICIOUS perfume for soaps in the bathroom and while there are many brands of rose-scented soap available in the shops, it is both simple and satisfying to experiment with making your own. It can be fun to establish roses as a theme for the entire bathroom, with soap dishes, flannels, and towels all bearing rose motifs. Even a hair tidy can be filled with a fragrant rose-scented pot pourri.

### HAIR TIDY
*A satin hair tidy has a delicate filling of rose petals and ground orris root. If its scent begins to fade, strengthen it with a few drops of rose oil.*

### ROSY WASHBALL
*Make a washball (above) by shaping home-made rose soap into a sphere, then inserting a knotted cord into the centre. Mould the soap around the cord to secure it and leave it to dry in a warm place.*

### ROSE SOAP
*Grate a bar of unscented soap and mix it with a tablespoon of hot rose water. When dry, form it into small shapes.*

# BATH OILS & WATERS

HE PERFUME OF ROSES has been used to scent oils and waters since ancient Greek and Roman times. Attar of roses, a highly concentrated and prohibitively expensive distillation of gallica roses, is used in tiny quantities in many preparations, although it can be overwhelming on its own. Perfume is difficult to make, but the lighter and gentler rose waters, particularly those made from noisette and wichuriana roses, and from the leaves of sweet briar, are easy to prepare. Bath oils can be quite simple to make and the resulting fragrances are really heavenly.

**TOILET WATERS**
*Fragrant and fruity-scented bourbon and musk rose toilet waters.*

**Rose oil** *is made with attar of roses.*

34

### ROSE COLOGNE

*Steep 250 ml (8 fl oz) of very fragrant rose petals in 125 ml (4 fl oz) pure alchohol in a sealed jar for a week. Infuse 125 ml (4 fl oz) each of rose geranium leaves and lemon verbena leaves in 125 ml (4 fl oz) boiling water and leave to steep for two hours. Squeeze all the liquid out of the leaves and add this to the scented alcohol. Decant into a decorative, sealed bottle, ideally with a special sprayer attachment for quick and easy use.*

### ROSE BATH SALTS

*Add several drops of rose oil to a jar of plain bath salts to give a lovely floral scent to your bath water.*

### ROSE BATH OIL

*Mix 75 ml (2¹/₂ fl oz) sunflower oil with 1 tablespoon of herbal shampoo and 2 tablespoons of rose oil in a bottle. Stopper and shake well Leave for two weeks, shaking daily.*

# A TASTE OF ROSES

THERE ARE MANY WAYS TO USE ROSES in the kitchen. You can crystallize their petals (see page 38), use rose water to flavour lemon and port jellies, cakes and icings, cold soufflés and ice creams, as well as sweetmeats, such as Turkish delight and marzipan. Richly fragrant petals make delicious jams and preserves, especially when lemon is added to bring out the rose flavour. The fruits and hips also make quenching drinks.

### ROSEHIP TEA
*Grind the dried rosehips and infuse in boiling water to make a rosy infusion, or mix with tea for a stronger brew.*

### TURKISH DELIGHT
*Boil the juice and rind of 1 lemon with 450 g (1 lb) sugar, 2 tablespoons rose water and 125 ml (¼ pt) water. Add 25 g (1 oz) soaked leaf gelatin. Cool in a wet tin; dust with icing sugar.*

### ROSEHIP SYRUP

*Pulp 450 g (1 lb) rosehips and boil in 1 litre (2 pt) water for five minutes. Drain the liquid through muslin. Add 300 g (³/4 lb) sugar to the strained liquid and boil hard for five minutes, until the syrup thickens. Allow to cool and then store in a sealed jar.*

### ROSE WATER

*Scald 1 litre (2 pt) fragrant rose petals in 300 ml (¹/2 pt) boiling water for two minutes. Strain the water through fine muslin and squeeze out all the liquid. Discard the petals. Store the cooled rose water in sealed or stoppered bottles.*

### ROSE PRESERVE

*Scald 1 litre (2 pt) fragrant rose petals in 300 ml (¹/2 pt) boiling water for two minutes. Squeeze through a sieve and discard the petals. Boil with the juice of 2 lemons, 450 g (1 lb) sugar, and 500 ml (1 pt) rose petals until setting point is reached.*

# CRYSTALLIZING

RYSTALLIZED ROSE PETALS taste delicious and look fabulous on gateaux and cakes. The best petals to use are those from the most fragrant roses. There are two methods of crystallizing, with different storage times. To make crystallized petals that will last for months, dissolve 15 g ($^1/_2$ oz) gum arabic in 60 ml (2 fl oz) warm water. Let it cool, then paint it on the petals with a paintbrush. Next boil 100 g (4 oz) sugar with 60 ml (2 fl oz) water until it reaches 80° C (150° F). When cool, brush it on the petals, and sift caster sugar over the top. The easier method of crystallizing below lasts for a week.

**CRYSTALLIZING ROSE PETALS**

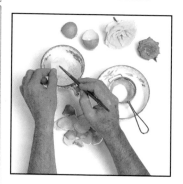

*1* Mix an egg white until runny but not whipped. With a small brush, carefully coat each petal on both sides with the egg white.

*2* Using a tea strainer, dredge caster sugar all over each petal. Place on greaseproof paper and leave for two hours to dry.

## CHOCOLATE & ROSES

*A rose made from thin, fluted chocolate adorns the top of this chocolate cake and is decorated with crystallized orange and pink rose petals.*

## FLORAL DECORATIONS

*Use crystallized rose petals to decorate cold soufflés, rose-flavoured ice cream, simple iced cakes, and home-made chocolates.*

# INDEX

# ACKNOWLEDGMENTS

**The author** *would like to thank the following people*
*for their help:* MAY CRISTEA, PETER DAY,  MRS P FRANKLYN, SARAH FRANKLYN,
JENNY RAWORTH, QUENTIN ROAKE, *and* N TULISSIO ANTIQUES

**Dorling Kindersley** *would like to thank* STEVE DOBSON
*for his help with photography.*

**Border illustrations** *by Dorothy Tucker.*